EXPLORING THE SUBATOMIC WORLD

Understanding
THE LARGE
HADRON
COLLIDER

Fred Bortz

Cavendish Square

New York

*To the thousands of unsung high-energy physicists whose work at particle accelerators
has revealed the wonders of the subatomic world.*

Published in 2016 by Cavendish Square Publishing, LLC
243 5th Avenue, Suite 136, New York, NY 10016

Cataloging-in-Publication Data

Bortz, Fred.
Understanding the large hadron collider / by Fred Bortz.
p. cm. — (Exploring the subatomic world)
Includes index.
ISBN 978-1-50260-552-8 (hardcover) ISBN 978-1-50260-553-5 (ebook)
1. Large Hadron Collider (France and Switzerland) — Juvenile literature.
I. Bortz, Fred, 1944-. II. Title.
QC787.P73 B67 2016
539.7'360944583—d23

Editorial Director: David McNamara
Editor: Andrew Coddington
Copy Editor: Cynthia Roby
Art Director: Jeff Talbot
Designer: Stephanie Flecha
Senior Production Manager: Jennifer Ryder-Talbot
Production Editor: Renni Johnson
Photo Research: J8 Media

The photographs in this book are used by permission and through the courtesy of: Fermi
National Accelerator Laboratory/Getty Images, cover; MichaelTaylor/Shutterstock.com, contents
page (and used throughout the book); © 1997 CERN, 4; © 2015 CERN, 6-7; Science & Society
Picture Library/Getty Images, 10; Source, Kurzon/File:Gold foil experiment conclusions.svg/
Wikimedia Commons, 11; Science & Society Picture Library/Getty Images, 15; Lawrence Berkeley
National Laboratory, 16; SLAC, 18; Topical Press Agency/Getty Images, 22; Keystone/Getty
Images (left), Francis Simon/AIP Emilio Segre Visual Archives (right), 23; Carl D. Anderson/
File:PositronDiscovery.jpg/Wikimedia Commons, 25; AIP Emilio Segre Visual Archives, Yukawa
Collection, 26; AIP Emilio Segre Visual Archives, Marshak Collection, 32; Science & Society
Picture Library/Getty Images (left), Georgios Kollidas/Shutterstock.com (right), 35; AIP Emilio
Segre Visual Archives, Gift of Kameshwar Wali and Etienne Eisenmann, 37; Source, Andres Rojas/
File:The Standard Model.svg/Wikimedia Commons, 39; File:AIP-Sakurai-best.JPG/Wikimedia
Commons, (top), ATLAS Experiment © 2008 CERN (bottom), 41; Public domain/File:SSC-
tunnel.jpeg/Wikimedia Commons, 45; ATLAS Experiment © 2008 CERN, 45; CERN, 48; ATLAS
and CMS © CERN, 49; Miguel Riopa/AFP/Getty Images, 50.

Printed in the United States of America

Contents

Introduction

Deep underground at the border of Switzerland and France near Lake Geneva and the Jura Mountains is a giant doughnut-shaped concrete tunnel. It measures 12 feet (3.8 meters) in diameter and has a circumference of 17 miles (27 kilometers). Within that tunnel is the largest and most complex machine ever built: the Large **Hadron** Collider,

Aerial View of CERN with the Jura Mountains in the Background. The large circle shows the line of the LHC tunnel. The dotted line indicates the the border between France (background) and Switzerland (foreground)

commonly called the LHC. (Hadron is the name of a class of subatomic particles, which will be described in later chapters.) That remarkable machine enables scientists both to study the subatomic world in ways no other machine could before it, and to reveal how the universe as we know it came to be.

The LHC is run by the organization known around the world as CERN, an acronym for its original French name, Conseil Européen pour la Recherche Nucléaire (European Council for Nuclear Research). The French word *Organisation* (Organization) has since replaced Conseil in its title. The giant machine is the latest and by far the most powerful descendent of machines first built in the 1930s.

Though scientists did not use the term, those early machines were commonly called "atom smashers." A better description would have been "nucleus smashers," but scientists always preferred a less sensational one: **particle accelerators**.

The first particle accelerators emerged in the 1930s at a time of great excitement in the field of physics, the science of matter, energy, and the basic forces of nature. Theories known as relativity and **quantum mechanics** had transformed physicists' basic understanding of space and time, matter and energy, waves and particles. Experiments had revealed that an atom is comprised of lightweight electrons surrounding

Improvements Made to Upgrade the LHC (2013–2015). (1) New magnets (2) Stronger connections (3) Safer magnets (4) Higher-energy beams (5) Narrower beams (6) Smaller but closer proton packets (7) Higher voltage (8) Superior cryogenics (ultra-cold liquids) (9) Radiation-resistant electronics (10) More secure vacuum

a tiny but massive nucleus. Other work suggested that the nucleus itself contained even smaller particles called protons and neutrons.

Physicists designed and built particle accelerators to explore the makeup of nuclei by blowing them to pieces. The machines bombarded targets with subatomic particles accelerated to very high energy. At around the same time, scientists studying cosmic rays, which are very energetic particles that stream down to Earth from space, saw hints of other types of matter that were

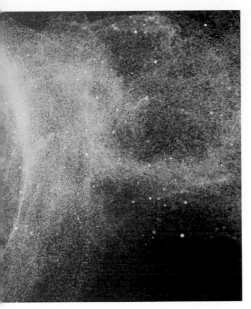

not found in atoms. That led to a new purpose for particle accelerators: besides smashing nuclei apart, they could create artificial cosmic rays.

Over the decades, particle acclerators have become more and more powerful, and they have changed our understanding of the subatomic world. This book is a journey through their history. It tells a story of exploration and questions—including questions that no one knew enough to ask when the journey began. It follows a path full of surprises, setbacks, and successes—including the triumphant discovery of a long-sought particle called the **Higgs boson**.

Yet as important as finding the Higgs has been, it is far from the end of the story. As this book is being written, the LHC is restarting after a two-year shutdown for an upgrade. A new adventure is beginning. This time the LHC is not only peering deep into the heart of matter, but it is also looking back to the earliest moments of the universe. Our journey will end not with answers but with a new set of questions—questions that may require bigger and more powerful machines to answer.

1 SPLITTING
the Atom

W hy are atoms like fiction writers? Because they make up everything!

That joke makes people laugh because when they were in school, they probably learned that all the matter in the world is made up of atoms. The word "atom" traces back to ancient Greek philosophers Democritus and Leucippus who were trying to understand the nature of matter. Those ancient scholars imagined cutting a piece of matter into smaller and smaller pieces until it reached a point where it could not be divided any more. They called that smallest possible piece *atomos*, meaning indivisible.

Their idea has been very useful in science, but, as we now know, it was only a starting point. For example, the smallest piece of matter that can still be called water is a molecule made up of two hydrogen atoms and one oxygen atom. And although those atoms are the smallest pieces of matter that can be called hydrogen and oxygen, they are made up of even smaller subatomic particles called protons, neutrons, and electrons.

Electrons are indivisible, but remarkably, protons and neutrons are not. Furthermore, scientists have found other subatomic particles that are not found within ordinary matter. To study the subatomic world, those scientists have built powerful particle accelerators like the Large Hadron Collider.

To understand the LHC and its discoveries, we need to look into the history of its smaller and less powerful ancestors, and we need to know how scientists first discovered the world of subatomic particles. We begin more than one hundred years ago in the laboratory of noted physicist Ernest Rutherford (1871–1937) at the University of Manchester in England.

An Astonishing Experiment

When New Zealand–born Rutherford arrived in Manchester in 1907, he was already world-famous for his work on radioactivity, first at the renowned Cavendish Laboratory at England's Cambridge University and then at McGill University in Montreal, Canada. Thus few scientists were surprised when his studies of radioactive elements earned him the 1908 Nobel Prize in Chemistry.

That prestigious award usually marks the pinnacle of a scientist's career, but Rutherford's most important work was only about to begin. He set out to understand the inner structure of atoms. He had been at Cavendish in 1897 when Joseph John (J. J.) Thomson (1856–1940) discovered the first known subatomic particle, the electron. Electrons carry a negative electric charge, but atoms are electrically neutral.

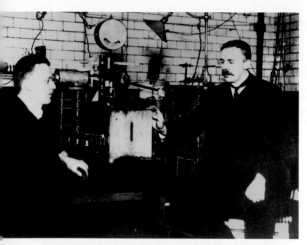

Ernest Rutherford and Hans Geiger. Along with Ernest Marsden, Rutherford (*right*) and Geiger (*left*) conducted an experiment that revealed the atomic nucleus. Geiger invented a detector that counted alpha particles one by one.

Therefore an atom had to contain as much positive charge as the total of its electrons. Furthermore, electrons are extremely lightweight compared to their atoms. The big questions were where most of the atom's mass was, and how an atom's positive and negative charges fit together.

Some scientists thought that atoms would be in the form of solid balls. Thomson had a different idea. He suggested that an atom was like a popular dessert called plum pudding, with the positive charges spread out like small fruits in a solid mass. Rutherford had an idea of how to test the various models of atoms. His approach was to send beams of a particular form of radioactivity known as alpha rays to probe large atoms, such as gold. He already knew that **alpha rays** were positively charged particles, and his early measurements at Manchester showed that they were helium atoms without their electrons.

Rutherford directed a beam of **alpha particles** toward thin strips of metal foil and measured the scattering, or the pattern of the deflections produced by their interactions with the atoms in the foil. From that pattern, he expected to deduce the size, spacing, and perhaps even the shape or internal structure of those atoms. To do that, he needed a detector that could count the alphas after they passed through the foil. His student Hans Geiger (1882–1945) designed and built an instrument, now known as a Geiger counter, to do that.

Rutherford and Geiger began their scattering experiments in 1909 and quickly noted that nearly all the alphas passed straight through the foil or deflected only slightly. That was exactly what they would expect from Thomson's plum pudding atoms, except for one remaining puzzle: a few alpha particles were unaccounted for. Had those particles scattered beyond the detectors? If so, what was deflecting that small number of alphas so much, while almost all the rest passed nearly straight through the foil?

Intrigued, but not wanting to divert Geiger from his detailed measurements, Rutherford decided that the task of looking for large-angle scattering would be good practice for Ernest Marsden (1889–1970), a young student just learning the techniques of research. Marsden found the missing alpha particles. Some went to the left or right of the original detectors, and astonishingly, a few even scattered backward!

By 1911, Rutherford was ready to announce his explanation to the world. He described atoms as miniature solar systems

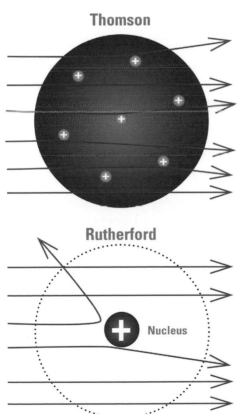

Thomson

Rutherford

Nucleus

Unexpected Results. In Rutherford and Geiger's experiment, most particles deflected only slightly, if at all. However, a small number deflected in unexpected directions—off to the side or nearly backward. Rutherford realized that Thomson's plum pudding model was wrong. Instead, he concluded that most of the mass of the atom was contained in a very compact central region that he called the nucleus.

held together by electrical forces instead of gravity. Most of an atom is empty space. Tiny electrons, like planets, have only a small fraction of the system's total mass and orbit a much more massive central body called the nucleus (plural nuclei). The nucleus is very compact. Its large mass and positive charge are concentrated in about one ten-thousandth of the diameter of the atom. The emptiness of the atom explains why most alpha particles pass through it with little scattering. But on those rare occasions when a fast-moving alpha particle makes a nearly direct hit on a heavy nucleus, the alpha scatters sideways or even backward.

Inside the Nucleus

But is the nucleus a fundamental particle? Rutherford and other scientists thought not. Nature seemed to have a basic unit of electric charge, and so most scientists thought that the nucleus would probably contain as many positive particles, which they called protons, as the atom had electrons.

However, by looking at the periodic table of the elements they quickly realized that things were not quite so simple. The atomic weight—or atomic mass, a term physicists prefer—of hydrogen is one. Its atomic number is also one. However, helium, with atomic number two, has an atomic mass of four hydrogen atoms (or four atomic mass units). Further up the periodic table, the problem is worse. Lead, for example, has atomic number 82 and atomic mass 207. Protons did not account for even half the mass of most nuclei.

Rutherford reflected on the situation, and he realized that the extra mass might have something to do with another question. Bodies with the same kind of electric charge repel each other, and the force between them becomes much more powerful as they get closer together. Containing so many positively charged protons packed close together, the nucleus would blow itself to bits, or so it seemed. Whatever is giving the nucleus extra mass must also be responsible for holding the nucleus together. Rutherford theorized that the rest of the mass came from electrically neutral particles with masses about the same as protons. He called them neutrons, and he turned out to be right (although they were not detected until 1932).

The discovery of the neutron established the basic atomic structure we now know: a tiny but massive nucleus of positively charged protons and electrically neutral neutrons, occupying only about a ten-thousandth of the atom's diameter, surrounded by light electrons in equal number to the protons. Still, many questions remained about atoms and subatomic particles, including the nature of radioactivity and the powerful nuclear force that binds the nucleus together.

Splitting the Nucleus

Rutherford was not only a great scientist in his own right, he was also a great leader of others. In 1919, he succeeded J. J. Thomson as director of the Cavendish Laboratory. There, under his leadership in 1932, James Chadwick (1891–1974) confirmed Rutherford's instincts and discovered neutrons. That discovery earned Chadwick the Nobel Prize for Physics in 1935.

Another Nobel Prize–winning experiment was also under way at the Cavendish at that time. John Cockcroft (1897–1967) and Ernest Walton (1903–1995) had designed and built a device that used high voltage to acclerate protons toward a target through a tube measuring 8 feet (2.4 m) long. To keep the protons from unwanted collisions with gas molecules, they needed a vacuum pump to remove almost all the air from the tube. They hoped they could eventually accelerate protons to a high enough energy to break a nucleus apart. They didn't think their machine was ready when Rutherford marched into their laboratory on a Wednesday morning in April 1932. He told them to stop fiddling with the design and to see what their machine was capable of.

When Rutherford spoke, people listened. It was not because he intimidated them, though his large stature and booming voice commanded attention. It was because Rutherford's colleagues knew that his scientific instincts were usually right. So Cockcroft and Walton wasted no time putting a lithium foil target in place along with a zinc sulfide screen to detect whatever activity would result. When they turned on their apparatus the next day, they made history.

The lithium nuclei in their target had three protons and four neutrons. When a high-energy proton made a direct hit on a lithium nucleus, it penetrated the nucleus, resulting in four protons and four neutrons. Those quickly reassembled into two alpha particles (two protons and two neutrons each). The Cavendish team had won an international race to be first to split a nucleus. It earned them a Nobel Prize in 1951.

One of their competitors in that race was Ernest O. Lawrence (1901–1958) at the University of California, Berkeley. Rather than using a long tube, Lawrence devised a more compact device called a **cyclotron** with a disk-shaped vacuum chamber. The disk was divided by a narrow gap into two dees with an alternating high voltage across the gap between them. Protons or other particles were injected near the center of

An Unexpected Success

Cockcroft and Walton did not expect their proton accelerator to be successful at splitting the lithium nucleus. They thought it would take much more energy to break it apart than their accelerator could deliver. They did not count on the special nature of alpha particles. That combination of two protons and two neutrons is the most tightly bound of all nuclei. Inside a nucleus, the protons and neutrons are constantly rearranging themselves. So a lithium nucleus, with its three protons and four neutrons, often looks like it contains an alpha particle plus a proton and two neutrons.

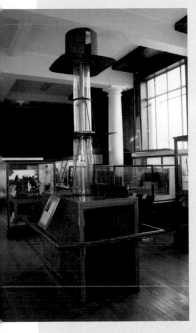

The two scientists anticipated that an accelerated proton in their apparatus could make a direct hit on a lithium nucleus and combine with one of its protons and two of its neutrons to make a second alpha particle. They knew how much energy it would take to penetrate the nucleus, and that was more than their accelerator could deliver. Thus they were surprised when they managed to split that lithium nucleus.

Why did it take less energy than expected? The proton didn't need to penetrate the nucleus completely. If it got close enough, the tendency of protons and neutrons to bind into alpha particles enabled it to combine with one of the protons and two of the neutrons in the lithium nucleus to form an alpha particle. When that happened, the nucleus split.

Cockcroft and Walton's Proton Accelerator. Now a museum exhibit, the apparatus that Ernest Walton and John Cockcroft used when they became the first scientists to "split the atom" consisted of a vertical tube through which they accelerated protons downward into a chamber. Inside the chamber were a lithium foil target and a zinc oxide detection screen.

the chamber. The voltage accelerated the particle across the gap from one dee into the other.

A powerful magnetic field caused the particle to follow a tight circular path, which brought it back to the gap just as the voltage switched to the opposite direction. Every time it crossed the gap, it got a boost of energy from the high voltage. Its higher speed made it move in a larger circle. After a large number of gap-crossings, it reached the outer edge of the dees, where it was sent toward the target.

Once the cyclotron succeeded, it became the preferred design for particle acceleration for many years. It earned Lawrence the 1939 Nobel Prize for Physics, twelve years before Cockcroft and Walton won theirs.

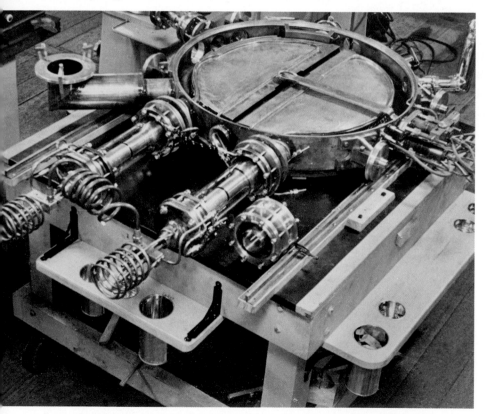

An Early Cyclotron. This 1936 photo shows the main chamber of a 37-inch (93.9 cm) cyclotron, divided into its two dees.

Types of Particle Accelerators

The race to split the nucleus had led to two basic designs for particle accelerators: linear accelerators, which shoot particles in a straight line, and cyclotrons. Both types had their advantages and disadvantages, and as particle accelators became more powerful, both contributed to the exploration of the subatomic world.

Cockcroft and Walton's device was a linear accelerator. Linear accelerators have the advantage of not needing powerful magnetic fields to guide particles as they speed up. One way to produce higher energies is to make a row of several linear accelerators, one after the other. Another way is to use higher voltages. As linear accelerators have advanced, both techniques have been used. Linear accelerators incorporated the most advanced high-voltage technology, but they also grew longer and longer. The longest is 2 miles (3.2 km) in length, and it is located at the Stanford Linear Accelerator Center (SLAC) in California.

Finding a site for a long tube is one problem for linear accelerators. Building it is another. SLAC's main accelerator is a tube buried 30 feet (9 m) underground, and it has to be perfectly straight. The builders even had to take account of Earth's curvature, which is about 2.5 inches (6.4 centimeters) per mile!

Circular machines like cyclotrons can be more compact, but they also have issues in their design, including both size and voltage. Even with the best high-voltage technology, accelerating particles to higher energy requires more trips across the gap. That means having either larger machines (allowing for larger circles) or higher magnetic fields to keep the circles tighter at high energy.

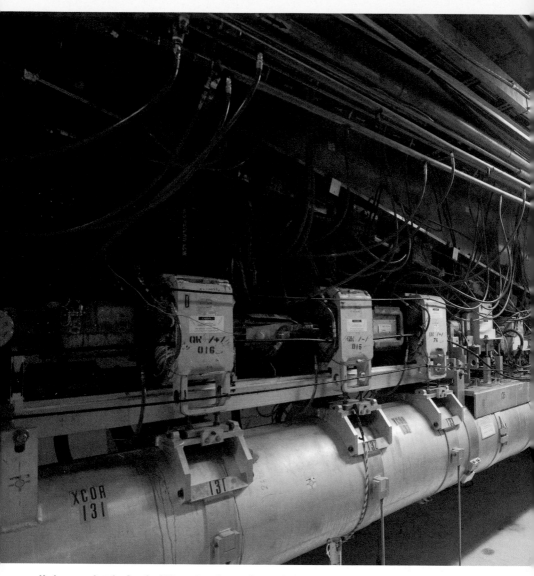

Underground at the Stanford Linear Accelerator Center. A worker inspects part of the 2-mile-(3.21 km) long linear accelerator at the SLAC National Accelerator Laboratory.

The original cyclotron worked fine as long as the accelerated particles didn't get close to the speed of light. At those lower speeds, each loop around the dees took the same amount of time. The radius of the loop was bigger so the particle traveled farther, but its increase in speed kept the time

interval between gap crossings the same. That allowed the designers to keep the alternation rate of the voltage constant.

But once their speed got high enough compared to the speed of light, the time to travel around the loop began to increase, causing particles to arrive at the gap when the voltage was in the wrong direction. To solve that problem, the alternation rate had to change to synchronize the arrival of particles at the gap with the direction of the voltage. The new machines were called synchro-cyclotrons or **synchrotrons**.

The first linear accelerators and cyclotrons sent their particles into a fixed target, like Cockcroft and Walton's lithium foil. As you will read later, this seriously limited the useful energy of the experiment. To make the most of their acceleration, scientists began creating **colliders**—machines that sent two beams of particles toward each other.

The first colliders used beams of electrons and went into operation in the early 1960s. Soon, particle accelerators were revealing so many new subatomic particles that scientists started speaking of the Particle "Zoo." A visit to that zoo is the next stop on our journey to the LHC.

2 THE
Particle "Zoo"

Discovering that atoms are made up of protons, neutrons, and electrons was only the beginning of the scientific exploration of the subatomic world. In the 1930s, scientists began to realize that those three particles were not enough.

Their most important clues came from radioactivity and cosmic rays. The work of Rutherford and others during the late 1890s and the first decade of the twentieth century showed that radioactivity came in three distinct forms, which were named alpha, **beta**, and **gamma rays** after the first three letters of the Greek alphabet. They discovered that alpha and beta radiation were fast-moving particles, while gamma rays were electromagnetic waves similar to X-rays but with even shorter wavelengths.

Alpha and **beta particles** were quickly recognized as familiar forms of matter: helium nuclei (alphas) and electrons (betas). Still, there were major questions about what was happening inside radioactive nuclei to produce those particles and the energy they carried. Other questions arose about the forces inside nuclei that held protons and neutrons together. Exploring those questions with the new theories of relativity and quantum mechanics led to the idea that there was more to matter than protons, neutrons, and electrons.

Mass, Energy, and Radioactivity

The most famous equation from the theory of relativity is $E = mc^2$, which states that mass is actually a form of energy. In words, it means that E, the energy of a bit of matter such as a subatomic particle, is equal to m, the mass of that particle, times the square of c, the speed of light. (The square of a quantity is that quantity multiplied by itself.)

That equation is important for understanding radioactivity. One of the most important principles in physics is the law of conservation of energy. That law states that in any physical interaction or process, energy can change from one form to another, but the total amount of energy can never change. The discovery of radioactivity posed this question: Since energy must be conserved, from where does the energy of alpha, beta, and gamma rays come?

When studying alpha radiation, physicists noted that all the alpha particles from the radioactive decay of a particular nucleus have the same kinetic energy (energy of motion). From where does that kinetic energy come? The equation $E = mc^2$ gives an explanation. When a "parent" nucleus undergoes alpha decay, the result is a new "daughter" nucleus smaller than the parent in both atomic number and atomic mass. The daughter, with two fewer protons and two fewer neutrons, has

Transforming Mass into Energy

In 1905, Albert Einstein (1879–1955) published three breakthrough scientific papers that brought him fame among physicists and later in the world at large. One of those publications led him

to a result that is very important for understanding the subatomic world. Among the conclusions from the theory of relativity is this: mass (m) and energy (E) are two forms of the same physical quantity. The equation $E = mc^2$, where c stands for the speed of light, shows that the energy in radioactive decay comes from the difference between the mass of a nucleus before and after it emits an alpha, beta, or gamma ray.

Father of Relativity. Albert Einstein is often considered the most important physicist of the twentieth century and one of the most significant in history. He is best known to the general public for his theory of relativity.

an atomic number two less than the parent, and its mass is less by approximately four atomic mass units.

Based on your everyday experience, you might think the difference in mass between parent and daughter should be exactly equal to the mass of the alpha particle, but that is not so. Part of the mass of a nucleus comes from the "binding energy" that holds its protons and neutrons together. Binding energy has a negative value since energy has to be added to break a nucleus apart. Of all the nuclei, the alpha particle is the most tightly bound. Its mass is less than the mass of the two protons plus two neutrons, either separately or inside the parent nucleus.

Thus when a radioactive nucleus emits an alpha particle, some mass is lost. That lost mass shows up as the kinetic energy of that alpha particle. Careful measurements of the masses of parent and daughter nuclei have shown that the kinetic energy is equal to lost mass times c^2, exactly enough to satisfy the law of conservation of energy.

Energy is also conserved in gamma radiation, though it is harder to measure. Gamma radiation never occurs alone. It always follows an alpha or beta ray. In those cases, the daughter nucleus is in an "excited" state and then quickly drops to a state of lower energy (and less mass) by emitting a high-energy **photon** (a gamma ray).

Beta Detectives. Studies of beta radiation produced a mystery. The energy that beta particles carried was less than expected from the difference in mass between the parent and daughter nucleus. Wolfgang Pauli (*right*) proposed that an undetected particle was emitted as well. Enrico Fermi (*left*) developed that idea into a full theory of beta decay and named the missing particle the neutrino.

Relativity explained the energy of an alpha particle. However, in beta radiation, physicists ran into a puzzle. Unlike alpha radiation, the emitted beta particles do not all have the same energy. Instead, their energies can be anywhere in the range from zero to a maximum value. That maximum value is what would be expected from the lost mass. However, in most cases the beta particle carries off less than the maximum, leaving some energy unaccounted for.

In 1930, Wolfgang Pauli (1900–1958) was the first to suggest an explanation, which was further developed in 1933 and 1934 by Enrico Fermi (1901–1954). Pauli proposed that to account for the missing energy, another particle was also emitted in addition to the electron. Fermi proposed that in beta radiation, a neutron in a nucleus becomes a proton and emits an electron (the beta particle) plus Pauli's proposed particle.

Fermi gave that particle the name neutrino, Italian for "little neutral one," because measurements showed it would have to be electrically neutral and carry very little mass. Such a particle would be very hard to detect directly, but as physicists studied beta radiation more carefully, the neutrino became widely accepted—even before it was finally detected in 1956.

Pions and Muons

Besides studying radioactivity, physicists were also trying to understand the force that held nuclei together. They knew it had to be an attractive force between protons and neutrons, and it had to be much stronger than the repulsive electrical force between the protons—at least when protons and neutrons were as close together as they are in a nucleus. But at larger distances, the nuclear force had to be less powerful than

Antimatter

Neutrinos are not contained within atoms, but they are considered atomic matter because they can be produced when a nucleus decays. They are also not the only kind of atomic matter that was predicted before it was found. In 1928, Paul Dirac (1902–1984) developed an equation that combined the ideas of quantum mechanics and relativity. The solutions to his equation suggested that nature allowed for what came to be called **antimatter**. For every type of particle, his equation predicted an anti-particle with the same mass and the opposite electric charge. (Another property called **parity** is also reversed, which means the equation also predicts antiparticles of neutrons and neutrinos.)

Most physicists, including Dirac himself, considered that prediction just a curioisity until 1932, when Carl D. Anderson (1905–1991) was studying cosmic rays and detected antielectrons, soon called **positrons**. Other scientists had seen signs of them as early as 1929 but did not recognize what they were.

Like neutrinos, positrons are considered atomic matter. Antiprotons and antineutrons can form an anti-nucleus, which can be surrounded by positrons to form an antimatter atom.

First Detection of Antimatter. Carl Anderson published this image of the passage of a particle through a thin lead plate in a cloud chamber. The direction of its curve indicates that it is positively charged. In all other aspects, the trail matched what is normally seen for an electron. He concluded that he had detected a particle that until then only existed in theory: the positron.

Yukawa Accepting the 1949 Nobel Prize for Physics. Hideki Yukawa's insights led to an understanding of the strong nuclear force as the exchange of particles that he called mesotrons between protons and neutrons. We now call those particles pions.

electromagnetic forces. Otherwise, the whole universe would be drawn together into one huge nucleus.

In 1935, Hideki Yukawa (1907–1981) of Japan came up with an idea that could explain that force, which physicists call the **strong nuclear force** or **strong interaction**. (A second nuclear force, called the **weak nuclear force** or **weak interaction**, is related to the process of beta decay.) Yukawa realized that quantum mechanics, specifically the

uncertainty principle developed by Werner Heisenberg (1901–1976), had something to offer.

Yukawa's theory stated that the strong force was the result of protons and neutrons exchanging particles inside the nucleus. His theory predicted that those subatomic particles, now known as **pions**, would have a mass about 250 times that of an electron. At first glance, adding pions would add mass or, equivalently, energy to the nucleus.

That seemed to violate conservation of energy—but that's where the uncertainty principle comes in. In physics, measurements always have a limit to their precision, which is sometimes called the uncertainty. Looking at the equations of quantum mechanics, Heisenberg showed that the uncertainty of the value of an energy measurement is related to the time interval used to measure it. If you multiply the energy uncertainty by the time interval, you get a value known as Planck's constant, a basic property of nature that appears in the mathematics and measurements of quantum mechanical phenomena.

Yukawa realized that if a time interval is very short, such as the time it takes light to cross the nucleus, the uncertainty of the particle's energy can be as large as the mass of a pion. In that case, the pion is considered a **virtual particle**, but it can become real by adding enough energy to a nucleus to release it. So the pion, though not yet discovered, joined the neutrino on the list of subatomic particles. Of course, scientists began looking for pions right away. The most likely place to find them was in cosmic rays.

In 1936 at the California Institute of Techology, Carl D. Anderson (who won the Nobel Prize in Physics that year for his 1932 discovery of antielectrons, as described in "Antimatter" on page 25) and Seth Neddermeyer (1907–1988) discovered

Not on the Menu

When Anderson and Neddermeyer discovered the muon, famous physicist Isadore Isaac Rabi (1898–1988) quipped, "Who ordered that?" He was referring to the fact that muons are not part of atoms but are otherwise the same as heavy electrons. That question reflects the joy that scientists feel on those rare occasions when their research turns up something totally unexpected. Events such as that send them down paths they never expected and occasionally lead to significant new ideas and phenomena.

cosmic ray particles that had about the expected mass of Yukawa's pion. But those particles didn't have the other properties that Yukawa expected pions to have. Instead, they looked like electrons in every way except for their heavier mass. They were what we now call **muons**.

As detection techniques improved, scientists continued to look for unknown subatomic particles in cosmic rays. Yukawa's proposed pions were finally detected in 1947.

Strange Matter

The subatomic world was growing, but it was becoming clear that cosmic ray studies were limited by the small number of events that could be observed. Furthermore, those events were not predictable since they depended on the random arrival of high-energy particles from space.

Particle accelerators offered a way to create artificial cosmic rays. The events were not only more numerous, but they also were easier to detect because they happened in an expected time and place. Thus thanks to advances in particle accelerators and detectors, the decades of the 1950s through the 1970s were filled with discoveries of new subatomic particles named after various letters of the Greek or Latin alphabets.

Some of those particles were created when an accelerated beam hit a target. Those particles would often decay into other particles with less mass. By observing tracks that particles created in detectors, physicists were able to analyze a wide range of subatomic processes.

Part of that analysis used conservation laws. These included conservation of energy (including the energy of mass according to $E = mc^2$), conservation of electric charge, and conservation of other quantum mechanical properties (including one called **spin** whose importance will be explained in Chapter 3). In interactions governed by the strong nuclear force, some expected transformations did not happen. One explanation of the missing transformations, according to Murray Gell-Mann (1929–) and Kazuhiko Nishijima (1926–2009), was that a previously unknown quantum property also had to be conserved.

They decided to call that property **strangeness**. Protons, neutrons, and pions had strangeness of 0. Kaons and other particles called lambda, sigma, and delta had strangeness of 1. Their antiparticles had strangeness of –1. Xi particles had a strangeness of 2, and their antiparticles had strangeness of –2.

Quarks, Leptons, and the Standard Model

As the number of subatomic particles grew, physicists began speaking of a particle "zoo." Every member of that zoo was related to protons, neutrons, electrons, and neutrinos in certain ways, but it was difficult to find a way to organize them.

In many ways, the subatomic zoo resembled the list chemical elements a century earlier. In the mid-ninetenth century, chemists were finding new chemical elements at a rapid pace. By 1869, the number had grown to 69. That was when Russian chemist Dmitry Mendeleyev (1834–1907) found a way to organize them in rows and columns using a property known as valence. His pattern became known as the periodic table of the elements, and it is still so valuable that a modern version is posted on the wall of many physics and chemistry laboratories and classrooms.

It seemed that a twentieth-century visionary like Mendeleyev was needed to organize the zoo, and Gell-Mann filled that role. In 1961, Gell-Mann and amateur physicist Yuval Ne'eman (1925–2006), a colonel in the Israeli army, envisioned a mathematical pattern of subatomic particles that included groupings of eight. Gell-Mann called it the Eightfold Way based on a term from Buddhism, the Eightfold Noble Path.

That was only a starting point. It took several decades to figure out what made the properties of the chemical elements follow Mendeleyev's pattern. The reason, as we now know, results from atoms being composed of subatomic particles: protons, neutrons, and electrons. So Gell-Mann asked himself whether the Eightfold Way resulted from some subatomic particles having even smaller particles within them. He proposed that protons, neutrons, and strange particles all are composed of smaller entities that he called **quarks**.

According to his theory, those quarks came in three "flavors": up, down, and strange. Quarks also had a property called **color,** which had nothing to do with the visual meaning of the word. They could be red, green, or blue. Antiquarks could be anti-red, anti-green, or anti-blue. Quarks joined together to make a white composite particle—either a triplet particle containing one quark of each color, or a quark-antiquark pair that had corresponding colors and anti-colors.

According to that theory, protons are comprised of two up and one down quarks. Neutrons are two down quarks and one up quark. Strange particles contain at least one strange quark. That explained the basis of strangeness. It is the number of strange quarks. The Eightfold Way predicted an undiscovered particle called the omega minus with strangeness equal to 3. In other words, it would be made of three strange quarks. When it was discovered in 1964, the Eightfold Way and the idea of quarks became the basis of understanding the subatomic world.

That was only the beginning of the quark family. Physicists now know of three other flavors called charm, top (or truth), and bottom (beauty). They group the six flavors into three pairs: up/down, strange/charm, and top/bottom. Any particle that is made up of quarks feels the strong nuclear force. Particles made of quarks also belong to a group known as hadrons, from the Greek word *adros,* meaning massive or large. So at last we discover the meaning of the middle name of the LHC.

The weak nuclear force transforms one kind of quark into another. As noted earlier, Fermi described beta radiation as the transformation of a neutron into a proton by emitting an electron and a neutrino. Once physicists realized that protons and neutrons are comprised of up/down quarks, they saw beta radiation a bit differently. It is the result of transforming a down quark into its partner, an up quark. When that happens,

Murray Gell-Mann (*left*, 1929–) and Richard Feynman (*right*, 1918–1988). Noted for their strong, quirky personalities as well as their breakthrough theories, Gell-Mann and Feynman were colleagues at the California Institute of Technology. Gell-Mann's discovery of the Eightfold Way led to the realization that protons, neutrons, and other hadrons were made of quarks. Feynman was one of the developers of the theory of quantum electrodynamics (QED), which is discussed in the next chapter.

it also produces two lightweight particles, an electron and a electron-neutrino. (The reason to call it an electron-neutrino instead of a neutrino will soon become clear.) Those particles are called **leptons**, from *leptos*, the Greek word for light or small.

Together, the up and down quark, the electron, and the electron-neutrino make up the first generation of fundamental particles in what is now called the **Standard Model of Particle Physics.** The second generation, which is heavier than the first, also consists of two quarks (strange and charm) and two leptons (the muon and the muon-neutrino). Likewise, the third and heaviest generation of subatomic particles has the heaviest pair of quarks (bottom and top) and the heaviest pair of leptons (the tau and tau neutrino).

By the beginning of the twenty-first century, physicists had very strong evidence that those three generations were all that nature had to offer. But what made one generation more massive than the next? In 1964, that question led physicist Peter Higgs (1929–) to propose a new subatomic particle, which now carries his name. Not everyone in particle physics agreed that his explanation was correct or that his particle existed. Still, the idea was important enough that physicists designed and built powerful particle accelerators to search for the Higgs boson. It was a search that would last almost half a century.

3 THE QUEST
for the Higgs Boson

Besides quarks and leptons, which are the basic building blocks of all matter, the Standard Model of Particle Physics includes a set of particles known as **gauge bosons**. Those are needed to explain the universe's basic forces or fields.

In our everyday life, we are familiar with two of those forces: gravity and electromagnetism. Studies of the subatomic world have led to two more: the strong and weak nuclear interaction. Before we envisioned subatomic particles and before relativity and quantum mechanics came along, great scientists had developed equations that described how objects interacted with each other.

One formula described how masses attract each other by gravity. Another set of equations describe how electric and magnetic fields produce both attractive and repulsive forces between objects and how those fields interrelate with each other to produce electromagnetic waves, including light. But at the level of atoms and the subatomic world, those equations needed to change. Relativity and quantum mechanics made physicists think very differently about how to describe the world.

Equations for Gravity and Electromagnetism

Before physicists knew about the subatomic world, quantum mechanics, or the theory of relativity, they used a formula developed by Sir Isaac Newton (1643–1727) to explain the gravitational attraction between masses and a set of four equations developed by James Clerk Maxwell (1831–1879) to explain electrical and magnetic forces and fields.

Although Einstein's theory of relativity and quantum mechanics have led to changes in the form of those formulas, scientists and engineers still use Newton's law of gravity and Maxwell's equations in their original forms for objects much larger than atoms and situations where speeds are not close to the speed of light.

Forceful Physicists. Sir Isaac Newton (*right*) and James Clerk Maxwell (*left*) developed equations to describe the most familiar forces and fields of everyday life.

New Views of Matter and Energy

Relativity took space and time and used the speed of light to join them into a single concept called space-time. That led to a different way to view gravity as well. Though it can be treated as a force in many circumstances, it can also be viewed as a warping of space-time by the presence of mass. Also, as noted earlier, the theory of relativity united mass and energy into a single quantity through its most famous formula, $E = mc^2$.

Quantum mechanics forced physicists to rethink the difference between waves and particles. In some circumstances, we can treat light as waves traveling through space. But there are times when it acts like a stream of particles that we now call photons. What is true of light is also true of objects we usually consider to be particles. Inside an atom, electrons behave less like particles and more like waves resembling the vibrations on a violin string.

Likewise, the equations of electromagnetism did not reflect the quantum mechanical nature of the subatomic world. Physicists needed a new approach. During the 1930s, physicists began to develop a new theory called **quantum electrodynamics**, or **QED**. When the theory was finally developed in full, it was similar to Yukawa's theory of the strong interaction in one important way. It relied on Heisenberg's uncertainty principle and virtual particles. That may seem like an odd way to view the universe, but QED has proven to be among the most successful theories in the history of physics.

Specifically, QED describes electromagnetic forces between electrically charged particles as the result of the

Fermions and Bosons

The subatomic zoo has a lot of different categories with different names. Some categories describe the relative mass of the particle. These include leptons, hadrons, mesons (middleweight hadrons formed from two quarks), and baryons (heavyweight hadrons formed from three quarks). The word **boson** comes from a different source. One of the quantum properties of a subatomic particle is called spin. Bosons are particles whose spin is a whole number times Planck's constant. Another set of particles called **fermions**, including protons, neurons, and electrons, have spin values that are odd numbers times half of Planck's constant.

The mathematics of quantum mechanics includes statistical analysis of those two kinds of particles. The names come from pioneering physicists who developed the appropriate techniques. Fermions are named for Enrico Fermi (who named the neutrino, among many other accomplishments) and are said to obey Fermi-Dirac statistics. Bosons are named for Satyendra Nath Bose (1894–1974) and are said to obey Bose-Einstein statistics.

Gauge bosons are associated with the fundamental fields and forces. They give those forces or fields their scale, just as a gauge establishes the physical scale of many objects.

Satyendra Nath Bose Viewing a Photo of Einstein. Along with Einstein, Indian physicist Bose developed the mathematics that describes the behavior of a class of subatomic particles, now referred to as bosons, after his name.

exchange of virtual photons. Those photons are referred to as the gauge bosons of the electromagnetic field. For the full meaning of that term, see "Fermions and Bosons" on page 37.

The success of QED has led to similar descriptions of the two nuclear forces. For the strong force, Yukawa's original idea was that protons and neutrons exchanged pions. But after the discovery that protons and neutrons are made of quarks, physicists changed the terminology. Similar to the approach they took in QED, they developed **quantum chromodynamics**, or **QCD**, (where chromo- comes from the Greek word for color) to explain the force between quarks. Quarks exchange gauge bosons called **gluons**, which results in the formation of tightly bound pairs or triplets. In nuclear matter, the triplets are protons (2 up, 1 down) and neutrons (2 down, 1 up), while pions are pairs of an up or down quark with an up or down antiquark.

Photons and gluons have no mass, no electric charge, and travel at the speed of light. For the weak nuclear force, things are more complex. In order to match experimental observations, the theory requires two different gauge bosons that carry the same electrical charge as an electron or a positron. Physicists call those bosons $W-$ and $W+$ (W for weak). In addition, physicists developed a theory that joins the electromagnetic force and the weak force together to form a single **electroweak interaction**. That theory correctly predicted an additional electrically neutral gauge boson, designated as Z (for zero charge). Unlike the massless photons and gluons, the three gauge bosons of the weak force have masses between eight and ten percent as much as a proton.

Because gauge bosons are important to explaining the fields and interactions in the subatomic world, they are a major piece of the Standard Model. Thus you will often see that model

Gravitons?

Theoretical physicists differ about whether to include gravity in the Standard Model. As noted, the theory of relativity explains gravitational attraction as the result of distortions of space-time by mass. Still, some theorists say that the attraction could result from the exchange of massless gauge bosons called gravitons. If they exist, gravitons would be very hard to detect. For now, they are nothing more than a hypothesis—and a disputed one at that.

illustrated as shown on page 40. The illustration shows three generations of subatomic partices, each generation including two quarks and two leptons. In addition, the illiustration includes the gauge bosons corresponding to electromagnctism (photons), the strong force (gluons), and the weak force (the two Ws and the Z)—plus the Higgs boson, which is the topic of the next section.

The Question of Mass

As the Standard Model of Particle Physics was beginning to come together, one very important question arose: What is the significance of having more than one generation of subatomic particles? Except for the different masses, each generation seems to be the same as the others.

But many years before the Standard Model began to take shape, physicists were already pondering another question regarding mass. In the early 1960s, the strange quark and the muon were the only known subatomic particles that

THE STANDARD MODEL

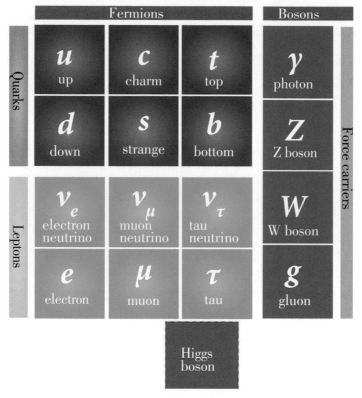

Completing the Standard Model. Physicists include the Higgs field and its gauge boson in the Standard Model of Particle Physics because they are needed to explain the difference in mass between each of the three particle generations. Those generations, each containing two quarks and two leptons, appear as the three left-hand columns of this diagram, with the mass of each generation increasing from left to right. The rightmost column includes the gauge bosons of the electromagnetic, weak, and strong forces.

were not related to atomic matter. However, by 1964, the theory of the weak interaction had developed to the point that physicists were confident not only that its two W gauge bosons existed but also that—unlike the photons and gluons of the electromagnetic and strong forces—they had mass.

That led physicists to ask not only about the source of the W bosons' mass, but also the mass of all subatomic particles. That year, Peter Higgs and two teams of physicists each published articles that proposed a way to answer this question: What is the origin of mass?

All three articles came to the same conclusion: the universe is filled with a previously unknown field. Except for photons and gluons, every subatomic particle interacts with that field to varying degrees. The stronger their interaction, the greater their mass. François Englert (1932–) and Robert Brout (1928–2011) were the first to publish (in August 1964). Higgs was next (in October), and his paper described not

Gauge Boson Pioneers. In 2010, long after the Higgs boson was predicted but before it was discovered, the American Physical Society awarded the J. J. Sakurai Prize for outstanding achievement in particle physics theory to Peter Higgs (in hard hat visiting the ATLAS detector at the LHC), who was unable to attend the ceremony, and the other pioneers in predicting the Higgs field (*left to right*): Tom Kibble, Gerald Guralnik, Carl Richard Hagen, François Englert, and Robert Brout.

Why Use Colliders?

As physicists strove for higher energy in their particle accelerators, linear accelerators and cyclotrons were no longer enough. They were limited by a very basic principle of physics: conservation of momentum. A particle's momentum is its mass times its velocity (including the direction of that velocity). In a standard accelerator, a high-speed particle strikes a stationary target. The impact may transform some of that particle's energy into mass as it produces new particles. But the momenta of those outgoing particles have to add up to the momentum of the incoming particle before the collision.

That means that some of the energy of the incoming particle is converted to kinetic energy (energy of motion) rather than mass. Because of effects of the theory of relativity, a larger fraction of the energy after the collision is kinetic energy—and thus not available to create new particles—as the accelerated particle's speed approaches the speed of light.

But suppose that instead of causing collisions between a beam of accelerated particles and a stationary target, the machine creates two beams traveling in opposite directions. In that case, when two particles collide, their momenta are equal but opposite and add to zero. All of the energy is thus available to create new particles. The disadvantage is that it is harder to create a direct hit in a collider because the particles in the beams are not as close together as the nuclei in a stationary target. The need to deliver more energy to create new particles makes a collider the overwhelmingly better choice, however.

only the field but also the gauge boson responsible for the interaction. Finally, Tom Kibble (1932–), Gerald Guralnik (1936–2014), and Carl Richard Hagen (1937–) added important ideas in November. Because Higgs was the first to mention the gauge boson, his name has become attached to both the particle and the **Higgs field**.

At that time, no one could make a firm prediction of the Higgs boson's mass, but as particle accelerators grew more advanced and the particle zoo filled out, physicists began to have a better idea. By 1983, the Standard Model's three generations were in place, though the top quark had not been detected. The Higgs boson also remained elusive, because without knowing the mass of the top quark, the Standard Model could not estimate how much energy would be needed to shake a Higgs boson loose from its field.

Finally, in 1995, physicists detected the top quark and estimated its mass using the world's most powerful accelerator at the time, the circular proton-antiproton collider called the Tevatron at the Fermi National Accelerator Laboratory outside of Chicago, Illinois. They were able to narrow down the range of masses where the Higgs might be found. They realized that with upgrades, Tevatron might be able to find it. But it was more likely that an even more powerful machine would be needed. That machine turned out to be the Large Hadron Collider.

4 DISAPPOINTMENT, Triumph, and the Future

The detection of the top quark came at a time that had been full of disappointments for the particle physics research community, especially those working in the United States. Two years earlier, on October 21, 1993, Congress cancelled the Superconducting Supercollider (SSC) project, even though more than two billion dollars had been spent and one-fourth of its underground tunnel's planned 54-mile (81 km) circumference had been dug, as well as seventeen shafts from the surface to the tunnel.

Even with upgrades to the Tevatron, particle physicists were not certain that it would operate at a high enough energy to produce Higgs bosons. Or it might produce Higgs bosons too infrequently to be certain about their detection. Thus the cancellation of the SSC boosted CERN's interest in building the Large Hadron Collider as the world's next big particle accelerator. Though the LHC would only reach 20 percent of the SSC's planned top energy, that would be more than enough

Money Down a Hole. Building the LHC was an ambitious project, but it would have been dwarfed by the underground Superconducting Supercollider (SSC) near Waxahachie, TX. After spending more than $2 billion, the United States Congress cancelled the project. This photo shows the partially completed and now abandoned SSC tunnel and one of the shafts connecting it to the surface.

to detect the Higgs boson, if it existed, and to go beyond to explore other big questions in the subatomic world. It would even have the potential to create conditions that had not existed since the cosmos emerged in an event known as the Big Bang.

And so, on December 16, 1994, CERN approved construction of the LHC. They already had a tunnel for it. Since 1989, that tunnel had housed the Large Electron-Positron Collider (LEP). In late 1992 and early 1993, three research groups developed plans for detectors that would study the results of high-energy hadron-hadron collisions.

By 1998, plans were complete for four detector stations. Excavation for those began even as the LEP continued to operate. When that machine finally shut down in 2000, the tunnel was cleared to make room for the LHC.

LHC Facts and Figures

Even with the tunnel already in place, building the LHC was a massive engineering and construction job. It needed to have separate pipes for two beams to travel in opposite directions around its 17-mile (27 km) circumference. It needed to allow the beams to cross at four different points, where particle physicists could place their massive detectors to observe and analyze various subatomic interactions and transformations.

The LHC is not perfectly circular. It has eight curved sectors joined together. Each sector has 154 powerful electromagnets to guide the particles around the arc. Those bending magnets need so much current that only superconducting wires will do. Electrical resistance in ordinary wires carrying that much electricity would generate so much heat that they would melt. Thus, the magnet wires are made from special materials that have no resistance when they are cooled to temperatures near absolute zero. To keep them at that temperature, they need to be placed in liquid helium.

Inside the LHC. In 2013, the LHC shut down for a two-year planned improvement. These workers are shown upgrading the ATLAS detector in 2014.

To keep outside heat from evaporating the liquid helium too fast, the walls containing the helium are surrounded by less expensive liquid nitrogen.

The pipes containing the beams can't contain any air, otherwise the hadrons inside them would collide with gas molecules instead of particles from the other pipe. (The hadrons are usually protons but some experiments use large nuclei such as lead.) The LHC thus needs perfect seals and very powerful vacuum pumps in every sector. The total volume that needs to be pumped free of air is about as large as the central portion of a great cathedral.

Since protons (or other positively charged hadrons) repel each other electrically, the beams tend to spread out as they move around their sectors. To keep that from happening, focusing magnets surround the beams. The LHC also has a variety of other magnets to control, shape, and direct the beams—about 9,600 in all.

The LHC is designed to accelerate protons to within 10 feet (3 m) per second of the speed of light. That is only about one part in 100 million less than nature's ultimate speed. At that rate, the beam can travel around the LHC at a rate of 11,000 times per second. Its beams are not steady. Instead, protons are grouped in bunches. Each bunch will have up to 115 billion protons and there may be as many as 2,808 bunches in the beam. That will produce as many as 40 million bunch collisions per second.

The reason for such large numbers is that collisions between individual protons in the two bunches is very rare. Most of the protons in one bunch will pass through the other bunch without a collision. Likewise, even when there is a collision, production of a Higgs boson is also expected to be rare.

A Shaky Start

The LHC started up on September 10, 2008, at much less than its maximum capabilities, like any other major engineering project. It began by sending protons in one direction, one sector at a time. Then it repeated the process in the opposite direction. The machine's operators gradually stepped up the power over several days.

Everything was satisfactory until a major failure on September 19. A faulty electrical connection between two magnets led to loss of control of the beam. It heated up the liquid helium, which expanded rapidly as it turned into a gas. The resulting explosion damaged more than fifty magnets and their support structures and contaminated the vacuum pipe.

The incident led to a total shutdown to repair the damage and to rework many connections to avoid a repeat. Finally, on November 20, 2009, the LHC restarted. Its energy was

gradually increased. On November 30, it reached a milestone, passing the Tevatron in beam energy. From that point on, it was the world's most powerful particle accelerator.

The management of the LHC gradually increased the power, but only up to half of

Early Troubles. Nine days after the LHC's startup in September 2008, a failure in an electrical connector like this one led to a major explosion that caused enormous damage to fifty magnets and contaminated the vacuum pipe. It took fourteen months to repair the damage and restart the giant machine.

its designed maximum, until after a short renovation at the end of 2011. That allowed a power boost of about 15 percent, which they thought would give them a good chance to detect the Higgs boson. They also scheduled a two-year shutdown at the end of 2012 for a major renovation that was necessary for full-power operation.

Higgs Discovery Diagrams. The LHC detected Higgs bosons indirectly by the production of other subatomic particles. The upper part of this image shows a pair of muons detected by the CMS experiment. The ATLAS experiment, in the bottom part of this image, revealed the Higgs by a set of four photons. Both events match the "signature" expected for the decay of a Higgs boson into lighter particles.

It's a Higgs!

After its successful restart, the LHC operated normally. At two detectors in particular, ATLAS (A Toroidal LHC Apparatus) and CMS (Compact Muon Solenoid), scientists began seeing hints that Higgs bosons were forming and decaying into other particles in the way the Standard Model predicts. Because those events were so rare, and other explanations were possible, ATLAS and CMS scientists needed to gather vast amounts of data to be confident that they were seeing evidence of Higgs bosons.

Finally, on July 4, 2012, CERN called a meeting to make a major announcement. Both the ATLAS and CMS teams had detected the Higgs boson using very different methods. Each had measured its mass to within a narrow range. Their mass values not only agreed with each other but also were within the predicted range. After a forty-eight-year search,

Award Winners. The discovery of the Higgs boson has led to numerous honors for Englert (*left*) and Higgs (*right*). Here, they speak with students of the University of Oviedo in Spain, where they accepted the university's Prince of Asturias Award on October 24, 2013, only sixteen days after the announcement of their Nobel Prize for Physics.

Higgs, Englert, and thousands of scientists from around the world who took part in the research were able to celebrate the discovery.

In 2013, Higgs and Englert were awarded the Nobel Prize for Physics "for the theoretical discovery of a mechanism that contributes to our understanding of the origin of mass of subatomic particles, and which recently was confirmed through the discovery of the predicted fundamental particle, by the ATLAS and CMS experiments at CERN's Large Hadron Collider."

What's Next for the LHC?

The discovery of Higgs was momentous, but the ATLAS and CMS scientists wanted to learn more before the planned

LHC shutdown. The managers agreed to continue operations into early 2013, but everyone agreed that the upgrades were necessary for the LHC to fulfill its promise.

Those upgrades included changes to assure that another massive and expensive failure, like the one in 2008, would not happen. The machine restarted in April 2015 and gradually increased its energy to the amount for which it was originally designed. That is where events stand as this book is being printed.

Subatomic physicists are eager to follow new questions and investigations, and they are looking ahead with great anticipation. The discovery of the Higgs, though exciting, is now history. It was also not a surprise. Its mass was in the range that most of those physicists expected. All they needed to find it was an accelerator that could reach high enough energy and create collisions in large enough numbers. Thus even though the Nobel Prize for the discovery was well-deserved, it was not unexpected.

After the restart, the LHC is entering new territory. No one knows whether new particles will be discovered and what their masses will be. Many are hoping another "Who ordered that?" moment lies ahead, because they have major questions to explore. Those questions connect the tiny subatomic world with questions about how the vast universe operates.

One cosmic question deals with **dark matter**. Observations of galaxy clusters and individual galaxies have revealed a great puzzle. They don't seem to contain enough mass for gravity to hold them together as they rotate. The best explanation is that galaxies contain more than five times as much mass of unknown "dark matter" as the normal matter in their stars and planetary systems. The Standard Model seems to be incomplete.

One popular hypothesis to explain the unseen mass is called **Supersymmetry**, or **SUSY**. This theory states that every kind of boson in the Standard Model has a supersymmetric partner that is a fermion (See "Fermions and Bosons" on page 37). Likewise, every kind of fermion in the standard model has a supersymmetric boson partner.

The predicted particles in SUSY are expected to be much more massive than their normal matter counterparts. The hope is that, if SUSY is correct, the LHC at its new higher-operational energy will be able to detect one or more supersymmetric particle.

Another major open question in subatomic physics is how the universe as we know it emerged from the Big Bang. The LHC's ALICE detector, which is named for its job of Analyzing Lead Ion Collisions, will provide some answers. For ALICE experiments, the LHC will accelerate beams of lead atoms that have been stripped of a large number of their electrons. When those highly energetic lead nuclei collide, they are expected to create a state of matter resembling what existed in the earliest moments of the universe.

Naming Particles in SUSY

Though SUSY particles haven't been found, physicists have had fun naming them. Some add an *s* to the beginning of the name. For example, sleptons include selectrons and sneutrinos, and the six flavors of squarks include, of course, the stop squark.

Others have been given the suffix -ino. These include the superpartners of the gauge bosons: photino, gluino, wino, zino, and Higgsino.

The LHCb detector (*b* for beauty) is expected to shed light on another major puzzle of matter. It will study subatomic particles with the bottom quark, because those are expected to shed light on the question of why the universe as we know it has more matter than antimatter. The Standard Model predicts that they should have formed in equal amounts.

The problem is this: A particle and its antiparticle will annihilate each other and produce energy in the form of photons. If the universe had equal numbers of particles and antiparticles when it emerged, they would by now have wiped each other out, leaving a universe of photons and no matter.

It is not likely that the LHC will be able to answer these questions completely. Scientists in many countries are planning even more powerful machines. These include the International Linear Collider in Japan, which is already being designed; a Chinese "Higgs factory" with twice the circumference of the LHC and a target date of 2028; and the VLHC (V for "very"), which would be three to four times the size of the LHC, which is in the early stages of discussion.

When those machines are operating, scientists are certain to have a better understanding of the subatomic world. They will also have a set of new questions to follow—questions that right now we do not even know enough to ask. But one thing is certain: higher energy particle accelerators mean that excitement lies ahead in our quest to understand the subatomic world!

Glossary

alpha particle or **alpha ray** A helium nucleus that is emitted from some radioactive elements.

antimatter Particles with the same mass but opposite electric chage and parity as corresponding particles of normal matter.

beta particle or **beta ray** An electron that is emitted from some radioactive elements.

boson A subatomic particle whose spin is a whole number times Planck's constant and whose spin quantum number is a whole number, such as 0, +1, −1, +2, −2, and so on.

collider A particle accelerator that operates by creating two high-energy beams moving in opposite directions and allowing them to collide with each other.

color In the theory of the strong nuclear force, this term is used to refer to a property of quarks that describes how they respond to the force, just as electric charge is a property of particles that makes them respond to electromagnetic forces. It has no connection with the visual color of an object or of light.

cyclotron A particle accelerator that operates by speeding up particles along a path of increasingly large circles.

dark matter A type of matter that scientists believe exists in order to explain the gravitational force needed to hold rotating galaxies and galaxy clusters together.

electroweak interaction An interaction between subatomic particles that results from a theory combining the weak nuclear and electromagnetic forces into one.

fermion A subatomic particle whose spin is an odd number times half of Planck's constant; in other words, its spin quantum number can be $+\frac{1}{2}$, $-\frac{1}{2}$, $+\frac{3}{2}$, $+\frac{5}{2}$, $-\frac{5}{2}$, and so on.

gamma ray A high-energy photon that is emitted from some radioactive elements.

gauge boson A type of boson associated with a fundamental field or force. It gives that force or field a scale to establish its strength, just as a gauge establishes the physical scale of many objects.

gluon A gauge boson that is exchanged between quarks, resulting in their being bound together by the strong nuclear force.

hadron A subatomic particle that is made up of quarks. In atomic matter, protons and neutrons are hadrons.

Higgs field and **Higgs boson** The Higgs field is a fundamental property of space that interacts with most subatomic particles to give them mass through the exchange of virtual gauge bosons. The field and bosons are named after Peter Higgs, the first person to propose a theory that included both of them.

lepton A subatomic particle that does not respond to the strong nuclear force. The leptons include electrons, muons, taus, and their corresponding neutrinos.

muon A lepton that has identical properties as an electron except for its greater mass.

parity A quantum mechanical property of a subatomic particle related to mirror reflections (similar to the fact that a reflected right hand looks like a left hand and vice versa).

particle accelerator A machine designed to accelerate subatomic particles to very high energies so they can reveal the properties of the subatomic world through their collisions and interactions.

photon A particle, originally called a light quantum, that carries electromagnetic energy, such as light energy.

pion Subatomic particles that are exchanged by protons and neutrons to produce the strong nuclear force.

positron The antiparticle of an electron.

quantum chromodynamics (QCD) A field of physics that describes the strong nuclear force as resulting through the exchange of gluons.

quantum electrodynamics (QED) A field of physics that describes electromagnetic interactions through the exchange of virtual photons.

quantum mechanics A field of physics developed to describe the relationships between matter and energy that account for the dual wave-particle nature of both.

quark A sub-subatomic particle that exists in several forms that combine to make protons, neutrons, and other hadrons. Quarks come in three pairs of "flavors": up/down, charm/strange, and top/bottom, and each flavor comes in three "colors."

spin A quantum number describing a property of a subatomic particle as if it were spinning on an axis. Quantum mechanics deals with wavelike rather than particle-like properties, so it is inaccurate to speak of a particle that actually has an axis and spins. Rather, quantum mechanics describes the particle as having a property called spin.

standard model of particle physics A theory that underlies the formation of all forms of matter and the fields and forces with which they interact.

strangeness A property of some subatomic particles. Scientists discovered conservation of strangeness when studying particle transformations under the strong force and later found it to be equal to the number of strange quarks a particle contains.

strong nuclear force or **strong interaction** A fundamental force of nature that acts on hadrons. In a nucleus, it holds protons and neutrons together.

Supersymmetry or **SUSY** A theory that predicts a not-yet-discovered set of particles that are matches to the known quarks, leptons, and gauge bosons. SUSY particles may account for the dark matter that seems to be necessary to explain the motion of galaxies and galaxy clusters.

synchrotron An advanced cyclotron that adjusts the alternation time of the high voltage to match the increasing time it takes for particles to complete a larger half-circle due to effects of the theory of relativity.

uncertainty principle A result of quantum mechanical theory that places a minimum size on the uncertainty of certain related measured quantities, such as time and energy.

virtual particle A particle that appears for such a short period of time that it does not violate the law of conservation of energy by more than is permitted by the uncertainty principle.

weak nuclear force or **weak interaction** A fundamental force of nature through which one type of quark transforms into another and is responsible for beta decay of a radioactive nucleus.

For Further Information

Books

Bortz, Fred. *Seven Wonders of Exploration Technology*. Minneapolis, MN: Twenty-First Century Books, 2010.

———. *The Periodic Table of Elements and Dmitry Mendeleyev*. New York: Rosen Publishing, 2014.

———. *Physics: Decade by Decade*. Twentieth-Century Science. New York: Facts On File, 2007.

Fernandes, Bonnie Juettner. *The Large Hadron Collider*. Chicago: Norwood House Press, 2014.

Green, Dan, and Simon Basher. *Extreme Physics*. New York: Kingfisher, 2013.

Hagler, Gina. *Discovering Quantum Mechanics*. New York: Rosen Publishing, 2015.

Marsico, Katie. *Key Discoveries in Physical Science*. Minneapolis, MN: Lerner Publications, 2015.

Websites

**American Institute of Physics Center
for the History of Physics**
www.aip.org/history-programs/physics-history

This site includes several valuable online exhibits from
the history of physics.

**European Organization for Nuclear
Research (CERN)**
home.web.cern.ch/students-educators (CERN Information
for students and educators)
cds.cern.ch/record/1165534/files/CERN-Brochure-2009-003-
Eng.pdf (Downloadable LHC Brochure)

CERN has an extensive online educational site, including
information about the Large Hadron Collider and the Higgs
boson.

The Nobel Foundation Prizes for Physics
www.nobelprize.org/nobel_prizes/physics

Find out more about every Nobel Prize since 1901. Read
the Nobel Laureates' biographies, Nobel Lectures, articles,
press releases, and interviews. Also, view video clips and
play games.

The Science Museum (UK)
www.sciencemuseum.org.uk

This site includes the online exhibit "Atomic Firsts"
(www.sciencemuseum.org.uk/onlinestuff/stories/atomic_
firsts.aspx), which tells the story of J. J. Thomson, Ernest
Rutherford, and other discoverers of the subatomic world.

Museums and Institutes

Ernest Rutherford Collection
Room 111 Ernest Rutherford Physics Building
McGill University
3600 rue University
Montréal, QC H3A 2T8
Canada
(514) 398-6490
www.mcgill.ca/historicalcollections/departmental/ernest-rutherford

The Rutherford Museum contains the apparatus used by Nobel Prize winner Ernest Rutherford when he was Professor of Experimental Physics at McGill from 1898 to 1907. The collection includes letters, documents, memorabilia, photographs of Rutherford and his colleagues, and other materials relating to Rutherford's work, including the desk he used in his home.

European Organization for Nuclear Research
CERN, CH-1211
Genève 23
Switzerland
+41 (0)22 767 76 76
outreach.web.cern.ch/outreach (CERN Outreach web page)
home.web.cern.ch/topics/large-hadron-collider
(CERN Large Hadron Collider web pages)

CERN, the site of the Large Hadron Collider, welcomes visitors to see on-site exhibitions or take guided tours. It also has traveling exhibits.

Lederman Science Education Center
Fermilab MS 777
Box 500
Batavia, IL 60510
(630) 840-8258
ed.fnal.gov/lsc

This museum is an outstanding place to discover the science and history of subatomic particles. It is located at the Fermi National Accelerator Laboratory (Fermilab) outside of Chicago.

Ontario Science Centre
770 Don Mills Road
Toronto, Ontario M3C 1T3
Canada
(416) 696-1000
www.ontariosciencecentre.ca

The Ontario Science Centre is Canada's leading science and technology museum. Its programs and exhibits aim to inspire a lifelong journey of curiosity, discovery, and action to create a better future for the planet.

Index

About the Author

Award-winning children's author **Fred Bortz** spent the first twenty-five years of his working career as a physicist, gaining experience in fields as varied as nuclear reactor design, automobile engine control systems, and science education. He earned his PhD at Carnegie Mellon University, where he also worked in several research groups from 1979 through 1994. He has been a full-time writer since 1996.